Heart of Hearing

Written by **Meaghan Thomas**

Illustrated by **Miriam and Sean Balsano**

*This passion project would not exist
without the support, encouragement, and love
of my wonderful family and friends.
Thank you!*

Heart of Hearing
Written by Meaghan Thomas
Illustrated by Miriam and Sean Balsano
Published October 2021
Skippy Creek
Imprint of Jan-Carol Publishing, Inc.

This is a work of fiction. Any other resemblance to actual persons, either living or dead is entirely coincidental. All names, characters, and events are the product of the author's imagination.

This book may not be reproduced in whole or part, in any matter whatsoever, without written permission, with the exception of brief quotations within book reviews or articles.

Copyright © 2021 by Meaghan Thomas
ISBN: 978-1-954978-26-3
Library of Congress Control Number: 2021949186

You may contact the publisher:
Jan-Carol Publishing, Inc.
PO Box 701
Johnson City, TN 37605
publisher@jancarolpublishing.com
www.jancarolpublishing.com

Author's Note

To the young reader who may struggle with wearing aids, please remember you are capable, deserving, and strong. Celebrate what makes you different and cheers to your ears!

The cat hears the cardinal chirp.

The cardinal hears the cow moo.

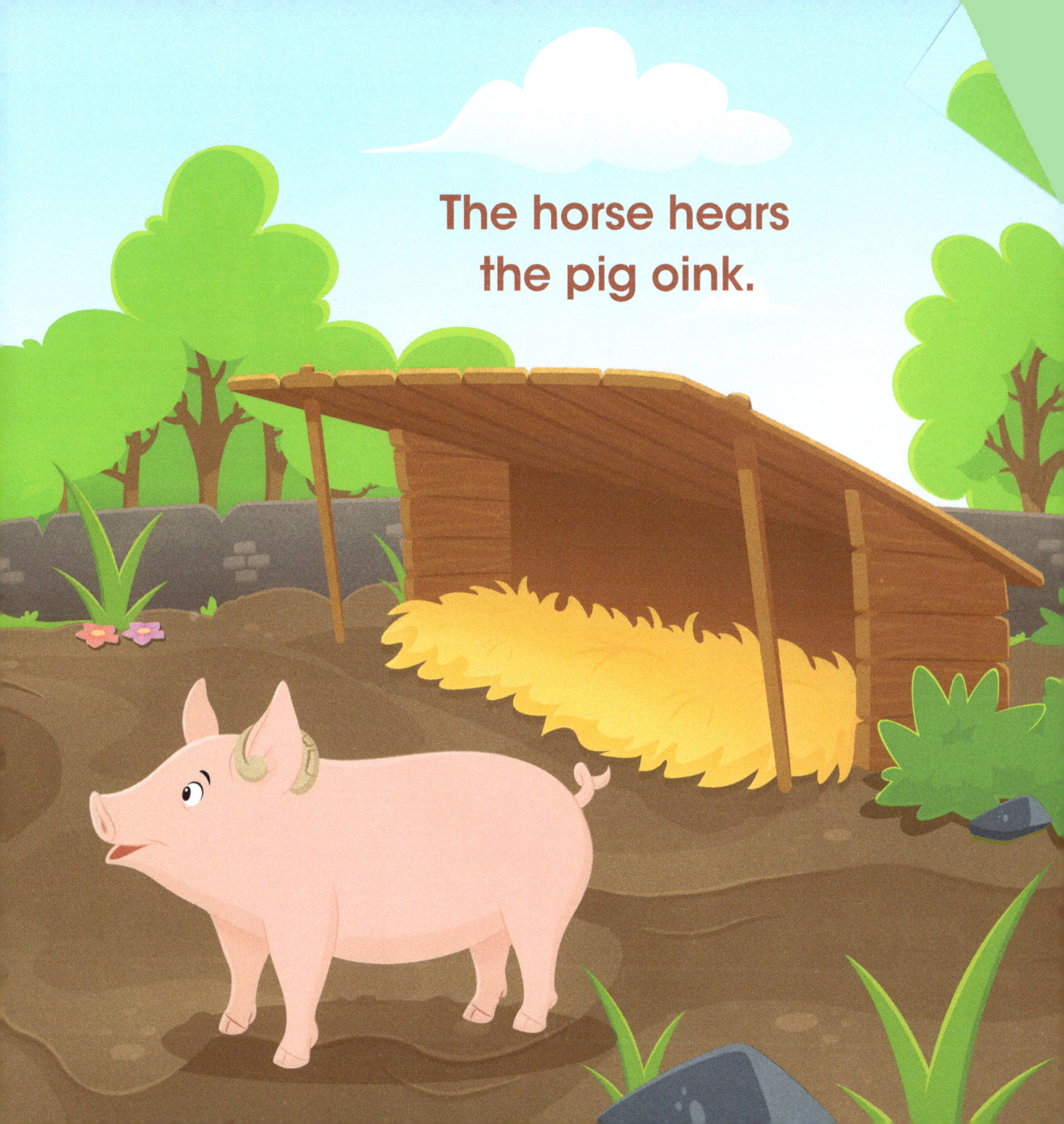

The bee hears the fish splash.

The owl hears the chicken cluck.

The chicken hears the duck quack.

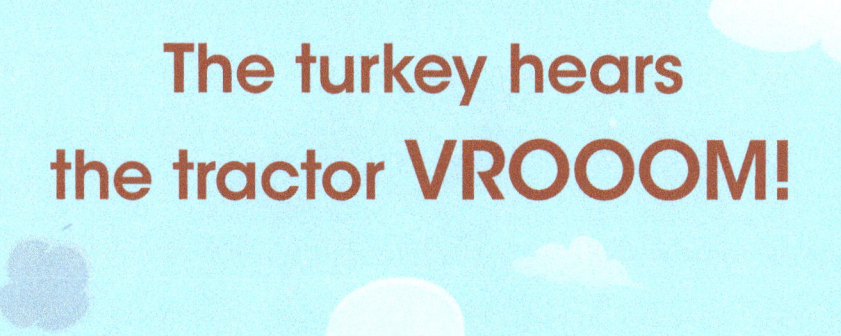

The turkey hears the tractor VROOOM!

I praise you because I am fearfully and wonderfully made; your works are wonderful, I know that full well.

– Psalm 139: 14

Acknowledgments

Accolades to my illustrators, Miriam and Sean Balsano. You brought forward my ideas and gave them life. Thank you!

About the Author

PHOTO BY CHELSEA ROCHELLE

Meaghan Thomas is an award-winning broadcast meteorologist. She earned her Bachelor's degree in Broadcast News and Geography from the University of Alabama and completed her Master's degree in Broadcast Meteorology from Mississippi State University. In addition to meteorology, Meaghan is a dedicated advocate for the hard of hearing; promoting awareness for the deaf and Deaf communities! Proudly wearing bi-lateral hearing aids, she hopes to demonstrate, encourage, and promote the idea that individual differences make you special. Her non-profit, *The Heart of Hearing, Inc.* will focus on increasing funding for those who cannot afford hearing aids. To find out more information and how to donate, visit: www.theheartofhearing.org.

- @megtomwx
  @theheartofhearingpage

- @megtomwx
  @theheartofhearing

- @megtomwx
  @heartof_hearing

- www.meaghanthomas.com
  www.theheartofhearing.org

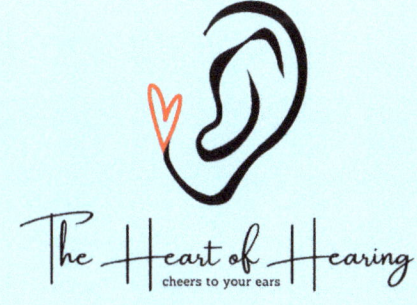

CPSIA information can be obtained
at www.ICGtesting.com
Printed in the USA
LVHW070419041121
702395LV00005B/19

9 781954 978263